8/09

TEEN LIFE™

FREQUENTLY ASKED QUESTIONS ABOUT

Academic Anxiety

Frances O'Connor

ROSEN
PUBLISHING®

New York

Published in 2008 by The Rosen Publishing Group, Inc.
29 East 21st Street, New York, NY 10010

Copyright © 2008 by The Rosen Publishing Group, Inc.

First Edition

Library of Congress Cataloging-in-Publication Data

O'Connor, Frances.
Frequently asked questions about academic anxiety/Frances O'Connor.
    p. cm.—(FAQ: teen life)
Includes bibliographical references and index.
ISBN-13: 978-1-4042-1937-3 (hardcover)
ISBN-10: 1-4042-1937-4 (hardcover)
1. Academic achievement—Psychological aspects—Juvenile literature. 2. Stress (Psychology)—Juvenile literature. 3. Anxiety in adolescence—Juvenile literature. I. Title.
LB1062.6.O25 2008
370.15—dc22

                                                    2007007848

Manufactured in the United States of America

Contents

Introduction

Every student feels stress and anxiety in school at one time or another. This stress might come from having to give a speech or presentation in front of the class, or maybe a performance in front of the whole school. Perhaps you feel worried every time you enter a very strict teacher's classroom. Maybe in the past you have felt stressed out while trying to complete an assignment in a subject that isn't your strongest area. Having anxiety means feeling stressed out, whether it's because you have a lot on your plate or because you worry that what is on your plate is done well.

The experience of feeling under pressure at school is not all that uncommon. School is where you learn new skills. The main way in which teachers judge how well you're learning and practicing these skills is by assigning homework, reports, and presentations, and by giving tests and quizzes. As if that weren't bad enough, all of these measurements of your new skills and academic abilities are timed. Trying to remember math equations, new Spanish vocabulary, or the formula of gravity during a twenty-minute quiz can rattle even the most relaxed person.

The feeling of being distressed, fearful, or stressed out as a result of school pressures is called academic anxiety. Academic anxiety is experienced most often during timed exercises and in situations in which students are expected to

Performing or presenting in front of an audience can be stressful. Here, a high school student prepares to address a crowd.

perform their best when the stakes are very high, such as on the SATs, or when in front of others. The way in which someone experiences this anxiety can range from mild, momentary jitters at having to read out loud in class, to a serious disorder in which a person experiences overwhelming panic and has difficulty functioning normally.

WHAT ARE STRESS AND ACADEMIC ANXIETY?

In order to understand the range of slight-to-severe academic anxiety, let's take a closer look at the different reactions to academic pressures.

Healthy Stress

Believe it or not, the normal feelings of stress that students experience because of tests, quizzes, and assignments can actually make them perform better. How? When a person feels stress, the amygdala, an almond-shaped part of the brain that controls fear and aggression, sends a signal to the body to release epinephrine, or adrenaline, which makes the heart beat faster and blood flow even quicker to the internal organs. Dopamine, the chemical that makes humans feel pain, is reduced. Called the fight-or-flight response, this surge of chemicals makes the senses sharper and makes

A normal amount of stress actually can help people concentrate and do well on an exam.

the body respond more quickly to danger while making it less apt to feel pain. People can see, hear, or even taste more clearly while they have more adrenaline coursing through their system. This response was probably what kept humans alive when they were battling it out for survival thousands of years ago against wild animals, and it continues to keep us safe from danger.

While science tests aren't dangerous in the way that outrunning a lion is, taking tests is still stressful, and the act of taking tests produces the same chemical response in the body to fight the stress of the moment. The fight-or-flight response is simply present so people perform at the top of their game during the stressful period. The chemicals stop flowing as soon as the stressful situation is over. In healthy doses, anxiety about doing well is what makes you study for tests and complete your assignments on time. Stress, a less healthy cousin of worry, is something that every student experiences from time to time because of schoolwork or major tests. Stress also can motivate you to do better if it's a very temporary experience and doesn't linger.

Unhealthy Stress

Second, there is the unhealthy, or severe, reaction to academic pressures: the mind can seize up and overreact to school pressures and cause a bodily reaction that knocks someone over like a tidal wave, making him or her perform horribly. The second type of physical reaction is the same as the more mild kind, except that the abnormal response causes the fight-or-flight impulse to keep going when the situation is over. In the unhealthy reaction, it's the overly worried, out-of-control brain that keeps sending signals to the body to keep chemicals circulating through the system, tricking the body into thinking that it's still in danger. The unhealthy reaction is considered a disorder because it knocks the normal order of physical response into a mess, or disarray. In a disorder, the anxious feeling stays with someone even though the stressful situation is no longer taking place, and other unhealthy behaviors begin.

Anxiety Disorders

An anxiety disorder is a disturbance in normal mental health function that has specific triggers, or causes. According to the National Institute of Mental Health (www.nimh.org), it affects as many as one in ten young people. If you experience severe anxiety, you are not alone in your age group.

While there is no condition called "academic anxiety disorder," there are anxiety disorders that can flare up or become worse because of academic pressures. Some types that typically affect teenagers include:

Generalized Anxiety Disorder (GAD)

Generalized anxiety disorder (GAD) is a serious anxiety problem. Someone with GAD feels afraid and worried all of the time, even when there is nothing to be afraid of or worried about. People with GAD tend to believe that some disaster is about to happen. Even if they realize that their constant worrying is not necessary or helpful, the fear does not go away. They can't relax. They may have trouble sleeping. Someone with GAD is unable to concentrate or focus enough to study for an exam. He or she might

A variety of anxiety disorders, including generalized anxiety disorder (GAD), can cause sleepless nights.

worry and worry about something happening to a relative who isn't even sick. People suffering from GAD can always find something to worry about. People with GAD may experience some or all of the common effects of anxiety, but much more intensely and more often than the average person.

Panic Disorder

Some people have panic attacks, which are unexpected and sudden attacks, so often that they live in constant fear of the next one. Repeat sufferers may be afraid to return to places where they had panic attacks, or they may avoid certain social situations because they fear the embarrassment of being seen by others while having an attack. Some never leave their homes at all. Many doctors and psychiatrists would diagnose these people with a condition known as panic disorder. Panic disorder—frequent, uncontrollable panic attacks—resembles so many other medical conditions that its sufferers often are incorrectly diagnosed.

Social Anxiety Disorder

A common anxiety disorder among teens is social anxiety disorder, or social phobia, the fear of being embarrassed by a social situation. The problem with being a teen is that social phobia is not exactly an unusual fear. So unless it persists for six months and interferes with someone going to school, to work, or out with his or her friends, doctors are reluctant to diagnose it. Sometimes teens who develop social phobia were shy as children. It really is pretty normal to be self-conscious as a teen (bad skin days, bad hair days, getting changed for gym when you've just put on some pounds), but people suffering from social anxiety disorder may blush, get the shakes, and feel nauseated when they have to answer a question in class, and they worry about it all the time. Or they may be fine in class but terrified in the lunchroom.

Obsessive-Compulsive Disorder (OCD)

Obsessive-compulsive disorder (OCD) is another anxiety disorder. People with OCD are troubled by persistent, upsetting thoughts (obsessions). A common one is the fear of dirt or germs. They deal with this by developing rituals (compulsions), with which they try to control their fear. Someone who has OCD and suffers from the fear of contamination might wash his or her hands so many times a day that the hands become inflamed and even bleed, and yet the idea of stopping fills him or her with terror.

Post-Traumatic Stress Disorder (PTSD)

Some teens suffer from post-traumatic stress disorder (PTSD). This is the modern term for what, years ago, was called "shell shock" when it was first diagnosed among soldiers who had survived bombings and other attacks. Now doctors recognize that any traumatic situation that involves great physical harm or the threat of great physical harm can trigger it. When people find themselves in situations in which they feel helpless, fearful, horrified, or life-threatened, they can develop this disorder. A teen who has been mugged or raped, or who has experienced or witnessed violence (the physical abuse of a parent or sibling, for example) may suffer from flashbacks of this event. So may the survivor of a plane or car crash. He or she finds it impossible to feel that the event is truly in the past. Some people exhibit PTSD symptoms even when they were not directly involved in a traumatic situation, but they were there as a witness.

Some common symptoms are nightmares or flashbacks of the event, avoidance of certain places or people who are associated with the event, emotional detachment from others, or jumpiness. The symptoms of PTSD may present themselves at various times. Some people exhibit symptoms soon after the traumatic event. In others, the signs might take a year or longer to develop, or a specific event, such as an anniversary, might trigger the symptoms.

Agoraphobia

Agoraphobia literally means "fear of the marketplace." Many people think of it as a fear of open spaces or a fear of going outside of one's home. Actually, this phobia is much more complicated. People with agoraphobia are afraid of panic, and agoraphobia goes hand in hand with anxiety and panic attacks. In fact, the term "agoraphobia" is sometimes used interchangeably with "anticipatory anxiety."

People with agoraphobia will avoid places or situations that they associate with panicky feelings. The place may be a public area, such as a shopping mall, or a room in one's home. Most agoraphobics have a "safe zone"—a place where they feel protected from anxiety and panic. Leaving the safe zone becomes terrifying and difficult. People with agoraphobia also may avoid situations that make them feel panicky, such as being alone or driving a car. Some suffer from recurring panic attacks, whereas others deal with anxious feelings without attacks. Some may be too afraid to ever leave their homes. Others may struggle through busy lives, always trying to hide the terror they feel inside.

The Link Between Academic Pressures and Anxiety Disorders

Academic pressures might contribute to a general anxiety disorder, panic disorder, agoraphobia, or even social anxiety disorder if left

Myths and Facts

Only students who get good grades and juggle extracurricular activities have anxiety about academics. Fact ➡ Every student experiences academic anxiety at some point in his or her life. It is not unusual to feel anxiety about assignments, tests, and projects, regardless of whether you are a high achiever or somebody who struggles with school-work. It is very important to pay attention to anxiety when it creeps into your feelings so that you can address it before it gets worse.

Stress is never good. Fact ➡ In small doses, stress is what makes you get your homework done on time and complete projects to perfection, down to every small detail. When managed, stress can be a great motivator, and it can disappear after the work is completed.

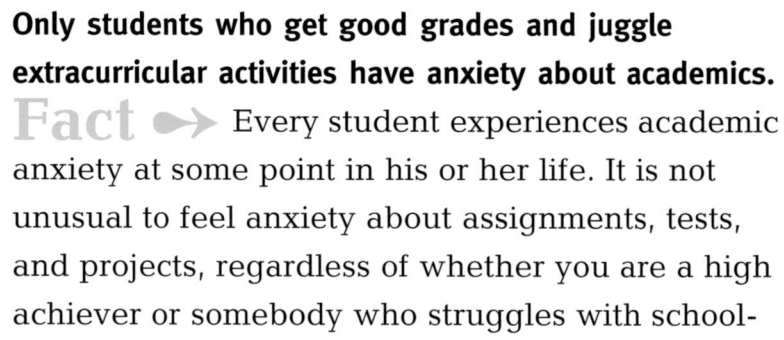

Myth **Preparing for college is the only thing I have to do right now, so I should take on as much as possible.** Fact ➡ Being a great candidate for a college means being a student who has earned good grades and has been successful at select activities and clubs. Colleges look at whether you are a well-rounded student who has made specific choices and excelled in academics. If you take on too many extracurricular activities, you might take important time away from schoolwork and run the risk of not performing as well as you would like.

Myth **If other people can't sense that I'm stressed out, then my anxiety is under control.** Fact ➡ Sometimes people can hide their anxiety levels even from themselves. It may not be until a person blows up at a friend or family member that he or she realizes his or her stress level. If you do this, or have the habit of hiding stress from others, it just means that you're pushing it down deeper, increasing the chances you'll feel more upset about life in general later. Identifying stress and talking about it are the most surefire ways to get anxiety under control.

untreated. The good news is that academic anxiety is readily treatable before it becomes a full-blown disorder. It is always important to know yourself and acknowledge how you are feeling. If you experience anxiety about schoolwork, tests, or presentations that won't go away, or if you experience any of the symptoms listed in the previous disorder descriptions, talk to an adult who will listen to your thoughts and feelings. He or she will help you find the help that you need from a trained mental health professional, counselor, psychiatrist, or psychologist.

WHAT ARE THE CAUSES OF ACADEMIC ANXIETY?

The causes of academic anxiety are different for each type of learner. If you are a gifted student, you might face the pressure of the high performer. Friends, classmates, teachers, and maybe your parents might expect you to be "on" all the time, meaning that you must always perform well and grasp new concepts easily and quickly. If you are gifted, you probably already know that being gifted means that you have special abilities, but like anyone else, you will naturally be better at some tasks and in some subject areas than others. This pressure can feel enormous in the face of homework assignments, activities, projects, quizzes, tests, and then high school and college admission exams.

If you are gifted, you also may have a different set of social and emotional needs that might accidentally lend

High performers and perfectionists can feel extra amounts of academic anxiety. Piles of homework to finish, tests to study for, and papers to write can all lead to feelings of stress.

themselves to increased academic anxiety. The National Association for Gifted Children notes on its Web site that "gifted and talented students may have affective needs that include heightened or unusual sensitivity to self-awareness, emotions, and expectations of themselves or others, and a sense of justice, moral judgment, or altruism." What this means in simple terms is that gifted students are more likely to be perfectionists—you are used to performing well and might be very hard on yourself to perform well all the time. The same desire to be perfect and the ability to envision a better world that frequently leads gifted students to be politically aware and involved in environ- mental and social justice causes, like preserving rain forests and helping their city's homeless population, can make them very hard on themselves for not being great at everything all the time.

If you have a learning disability, you might face the pressure of having to take extra steps to understand tasks before you are able to complete them. Whether it's using a reading strategy to understand certain types of questions on a test because you have dyslexia, or using a special method to take notes in class because you have difficulty transferring information from one place to another, your needs for an extra step in the process can make you feel anxious about school assignments and tests. Remember that if you have a learning disability, in most school situations you are allowed to take as much time as you want. If you are struggling to complete basic assignments and take tests in the amount of time given in class, you can talk to your teacher about your difficulties. He or she will likely be able to grant you more time and the resources you need to do well.

Reading or studying in a quiet place with few distractions can be helpful for people who have learning disabilities.

If you haven't been classified as having a learning disability but notice that you are having difficulty with reading and understanding class work, you can ask your teacher about being tested by the school psychologist or a learning specialist. While a lot of students assume that their teachers or parents would have caught their learning disability before they entered high school, this isn't always the case. Sometimes learning disabilities go unnoticed until the pressure-filled years of middle and high school because they're so slight, or because in elementary school there had been enough resources, attentive teachers who knew you well because they taught you every subject, and smaller class sizes. If you suspect you might have a learning disability, get tested. Knowing how you process information is a big step to lessening and managing the anxiety you feel in school.

If you are someone to whom the terms "gifted" or "learning disability" don't apply, you are still a unique type of learner, and it's important to think about how academic anxiety affects you. You might be more apt to identify yourself as an overachiever who takes all honors and advanced placement classes. You appear on the outside as someone who has it all together and submits all work on time or earlier. Or you might be a student who's barely making the grade who struggles to turn in basic homework and is running behind. You might be a student who performs somewhere in the middle of your class, but you might be surprised to find that you have high levels of academic anxiety in common with your peers whose academic performance is so different from yours.

Whether you are focused and successful some, but not all, of the time, academic anxiety can still gnaw at you. Here's a secret you should bear in mind when thinking about this anxiety: every student manages his or her time differently but still feels anxiety about finishing large amounts of homework and projects, and making school deadlines. Most everyone feels academic anxiety at one time or another, but it's important to recognize when these feelings are nagging at you constantly, even when no assignments are due immediately. If you have anxious feelings that won't go away, no matter how hard you work and how many hours you put in, and if you avoid tasks by putting them off (underachieving) or mix it up between working hard and coasting, academic anxiety is the bug that has bitten you. Hard.

It's important to address this anxiety before it grows too big and threatens to eat you from the inside out. You would never ignore a scrape on your knee that's gotten swollen and infected, so in the same way, you shouldn't ignore a raw feeling or wait for it to heal on its own. When you have a worry that won't go away, first identify it. Think about a couple of academic situations that were stressful recently, and write down a few notes about them on an index card or sheet of paper. Note the people involved, if there was time pressure, or if the work was too much. Additionally, quickly jot down your reaction during, and after, the situation.

Once you have this information down, read it again to see what it reveals about you. Do you feel more under pressure when deadlines are involved? Do you tend not to ask questions about an assignment in class, but then panic when you get home because you realize that you don't fully understand the task? Do you just take on the work a teacher assigns, even if you know you'll need help with it? Do you respond to a new project by thinking, "I'll never finish it in the time my teacher is asking"? You can solve your problems of confusion and time worries once you know exactly what causes them. The journey from a cause (worry) to an effect (relief from worry) is a pretty straight line once you've nailed down exactly what's going wrong. Take this information you've gained about yourself and go to a teacher, school guidance counselor, or your parent to talk about ways to lessen these worries when they first strike and when they hang around in your gut for a while.

A Family's Role

The pressure to do well academically frequently stems from home. Most parents are interested in seeing their children live up to their full potential and develop the best skills and abilities they can in the classroom. This pressure from parents can unexpectedly double if they have more than one child. If you are the younger child in the family, you are probably already familiar with the pressure that comes from being the second one to go to a particular school or compete in the same science fair that your older sibling did. Whether they mean to or not, your parents remember your older sibling's experiences and want to use those experiences to benefit you as you work on the same projects and assignments.

What makes parents' natural desire to help problematic is that you are your own person and have distinct needs, wants, and abilities that are separate from those of your older brother or sister. If this older brother or sister was particularly talented at learning new languages or math, there can be an increased pressure for you to perform as well as he or she did in the subject. If this older sibling was great at all subjects, this overachiever has left some very big shoes for you to fill if your parents are looking to hold you up to your sibling in comparison. If and when you feel yourself getting sucked into the trap of being compared to your sibling's performance in school, don't hesitate to remind your parents that you have your own gifts that you can explore and succeed in harnessing with their help.

If you are the older child, you may be expected to set a good example for your younger siblings. Your parents or guardians

If you are experiencing feelings of stress or anxiety, don't keep them to yourself. It can be helpful to talk to a parent or another adult you trust.

may expect you to do well in school, and this sort of pressure can cause anxiety. Speak to your parents honestly and sincerely about your feelings and try not to come across as defensive and angry. You should try talking to your parents about a request, rather than a demand.

Your Role

Overscheduling your calendar can lead to academic anxiety. It may not seem as if trying out for soccer and taking up knitting have anything to do with your science quiz, but they do. In spending your afternoons pursuing several activities after school, you may accidentally be putting all of your energy into those activities rather than studying. Parents also play a role in choosing which sports you play and clubs you join. They can recognize your abilities and natural talents and want to help you grow, but they might enthusiastically cheer you into a nightmare of too much work. By the time schoolwork rolls around, and you have had sports practice, music lessons, art lessons, and museum trips every day of the week, you have already spent your physical and emotional energy on the activities that are really meant to be extras to your schoolwork. Talk to your parents if you feel you or they have planned your schedule unwisely for the semester, and plan together to scale back on some of the activities.

Sometimes you might be putting pressure on yourself to join clubs, team sports, and after-school activities to make more friends or keep up with friends you already have. You might feel like these activities are the only thing you feel successful at thus far in life. Loading up on activities and clubs might be, in your opinion, the way to make you the best candidate for your dream college. If these are reasons that sound familiar, remember that you'll achieve none of these goals if the time spent trying to succeed in these areas makes you spend too much energy and spread yourself too thin. Too many extras can distract you from your true job—being a student. Determine if you've been the one to plan your schedule unwisely, and plan to drop some activities. Remember, there's always the next test, the next semester, or the

Participating in many extracurricular activities—football practice, piano lessons, orchestra rehearsals, painting classes, and more—can leave little time for schoolwork.

next year to do well. Rome wasn't built in a day, and neither was a great school career.

The best way to determine if a certain subject, task, or activity is causing you anxiety is to take your own temperature on this issue. Ask yourself: Do you feel worried regularly before going to this activity or class? Do you feel your teacher isn't giving you enough time to complete tests and quizzes? Do you feel anxious even when you're not doing schoolwork, but just when you're thinking about it? If you answer yes to these questions, it's a problem with a fairly easy solution. Have a conversation with a teacher you trust or your parents, and tell them that you feel what's happening in class is not going at the right pace for you and that you'd like to work in a different way. Teachers can be your allies. Creative teachers (and there are many) can come up with a learning plan that is unique to your needs. This individualized plan should help resolve some of the negative feelings you're having about your experiences in school each day.

WHAT ARE THE SIGNS AND SYMPTOMS OF ACADEMIC ANXIETY?

Whether you are experiencing mild or severe academic anxiety, you will have some inward and outward signs of worry. These symptoms are a result of the biochemical changes that take place in the fight-or-flight response. They are a means of the body holding up a red flag to notify you that it's having trouble dealing with a set of influences. These signs and symptoms can be hardly noticeable to the person experiencing them, though really obvious to everyone in the room.

Symptoms of Mild Academic Anxiety

- Dizziness
- Nausea or stomachache
- Sweaty, clammy palms
- Red blotches on the face

Worry—whether mild or extreme—can lead to a variety of physical and mental symptoms.

➡ Blushing
➡ Headache
➡ A rise in pitch of speaking voice
➡ Negative thoughts about failing the assignment or running out of time
➡ Self-doubt about abilities in the subject area
➡ Fear of embarrassment in front of classmates, friends, and the teacher
➡ Fear of failure

Symptoms of Severe Academic Anxiety

- Numbness in hands and feet
- Hypochondria (fear of getting sick)
- Inability to sleep
- Severe dizziness or loss of consciousness
- Difficulty breathing and feelings of being choked
- Paranoid thoughts of being judged by people or disliked immediately
- Obsessive, repetitive thoughts that are hard to stop
- Fear of feeling anxiety
- Fear of embarrassment in front of classmates, friends, and the teacher
- Depression
- Sadness and feeling weighed down by heavy worry
- Unending panic and upset that doesn't seem to be related to any one particular event

If you are convinced that your academic anxiety is off the charts, it's important to remember that it's common for everyone to experience some worries about school—worry or concern is a healthy emotion in small doses. The best way to determine if you are experiencing regular levels of anxiety about school is by talking to a school psychologist, social worker, or guidance counselor. He or she can ask you some questions about the types of anxiety you've been experiencing and can help you work out strategies for managing this anxiety. He or she also can help you sort out your own thoughts by repeating some of your statements back to you. This outside person is really helpful in identifying the degree to which pressures are at work in your life simply because he or she is not as close to your emotions as you are. This person is a key link to maintaining your wellness. He or she can recommend exercises to keep you feeling in control of this powerful anxiety that can otherwise make you feel as if you're drowning.

The "Trickle Down" Effects of Academic Anxiety

There are obvious connections between a person's thoughts and emotions and the effects they have on the body. There also are less obvious ways that academic anxiety can wear a person down when left untreated. Bodies rely on pretty complicated networks of emotions and thoughts. In the same way minds and emotions are connected to how bodies feel, emotions and fears about academics are linked to feelings about other areas of life. Like an overflowing faucet, academic anxiety can trickle out from school situations and down into other layers of emotions, where people store feelings about self-image, ability to have healthy friendships, appearance, and self-esteem. Academic anxiety can cause you to bring negative feelings to regular inter-actions you have with friends and family and cause these experiences to sour. You may start worrying about something a friend has said when joking around, or you might feel bad about a pointer your coach gives you after school. You might even take a parent's concerned comment to mean that he or she is

If schoolwork is creating stress in your life, it can help to talk with a friend who is in your class. Sometimes going over work or notes together will help you feel better.

angry with you. This is academic anxiety doing the talking, or feeling, for you. Simply put, you are still wearing the emotional glasses of academic anxiety and will see other life situations through these lenses of worry and defeat.

Academic anxiety can trickle down into daily habits, such as eating. Where you may never have had a problem eating your three square meals a day with some healthy snacks thrown in, academic anxiety can turn you into an emotional eater who relies on food for comfort. It is not that you have suddenly developed a poor eating habit out of nowhere. It's academic anxiety at your

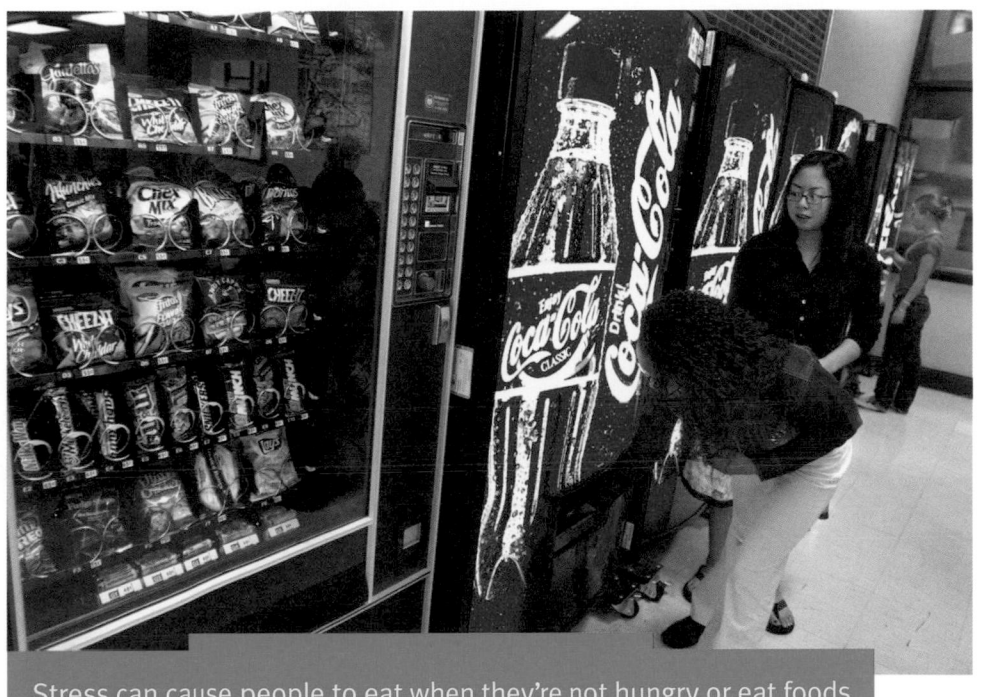

Stress can cause people to eat when they're not hungry or eat foods that are not healthy. This can be especially true for students in schools that have vending machines stocked with soft drinks and candy.

emotional center that is reaching its tentacles out and grabbing at your other emotions, twisting them into knotted negative feelings. Or you may be neglecting eating due to stress and other obligations.

Academic anxiety that's gone out of control can make you develop less-than-charming social habits, such as talking abruptly, interrupting others to talk about your own situation, or being absentminded about friends' birthdays and special events. Because you are feeling so worried about your performance in school, academic anxiety can put you through major mood swings.

Minor happenings such as the bus being late can make you feel as if your head is going to explode.

The good news about the symptoms of academic anxiety is that as soon as you identify what is affecting you, you have solved half of this complicated puzzle. Once you recognize that your anxiety isn't necessarily about the situation you're in, but about the powerful academic anxiety that's crowding its way into your thoughts from other life situations, the better off you are. You can take this self-awareness to that counselor, psychologist, or social worker and begin to work on ways to lessen academic anxiety's hold on your thoughts.

HOW CAN I MANAGE
ACADEMIC ANXIETY?

If you suffer from academic anxiety, there are a few helpful strategies you can use to ensure that it doesn't overwhelm you. First, know yourself. Once you learn that you are responsible for managing your anxiety, you will feel better about yourself. It may sound stressful to think about being responsible for your own education, but being responsible in this case really means that you can quickly recognize and cut down on the things that are making you most anxious. Understanding that part of responsibility means you have the power to reduce stress dramatically. When possible, think about your own learning style—the way you process information. Do you like it when you read first and then experiment with numbers or ideas? Do you like deadlines of a week or two? Do you do well on untimed tasks? Do you prefer working in a group to brainstorm

Whatever class-related problem you may be experiencing, your teacher or school guidance counselor can be a good first resource for help.

ideas, or do you prefer working alone to think about various solutions you'll later present to the group? Make a mental note of what works best for you, and carry this with you into each learning situation.

Second, know your school and teacher. Teachers are your allies, but not all teachers have the time and resources to help you manage the anxiety you feel when completing their assignments. Talk to a teacher who does have the time to listen to your needs. Let him or her know that you feel stressed out and what causes your stress, and he or she will refer you to someone like a school psychologist, social worker, or guidance counselor who can help you come up with strategies to work on any area of your studies that feels overwhelming. If you are a gifted student or one who has a learning disability and you feel that you are in the wrong environment, seek the assistance of the right teacher. The right teacher will help you come up with a plan that best meets your needs, and if necessary, he or she will recommend a separate class or program that might provide a more suitable learning environment for you. In the right environment, it's still your responsibility to be self-aware about your progress and to discuss with your teacher the best type of learning for your abilities.

Third, know your options. Health centers at many colleges provide their students with information on noticing and managing academic anxiety at orientation, and your middle or high school might have some wellness strategies listed in your student handbook. Usually available in the nurse's office or guidance counselor's office, your student handbook might recommend ways for you to stay healthy in, and out of, school.

Dealing with General Worries About Academics

The Cornell University Center for Learning and Teaching recommends using positive mental imagery to push away worries about school. Positive mental imagery is a technique where you think of a beautiful scene in nature or a positive image of yourself winning a game or having a great moment to replace negative

Ten Great Questions to Ask When You're Asking for Help

1 How do I find out if what I'm feeling is something worrisome?

2 How can my parents or siblings help me deal with my anxiety?

3 If I feel anxiety, should I ask for extra time to take tests and finish projects?

4 How do I know which situations are most stressful for me so I can work on performing well when they happen?

5 Whom do I need to tell that I have academic anxiety? What should I tell my friends when I need extra help in school?

6 Can I participate in pressure-filled academic activities, such as debating and giving speeches?

7 Are there support groups at school for people who feel really stressed out?

8 Why do I not deal well with stress?

9 How should I push myself to do better without putting too much pressure on myself to do well?

10 What should I do before I have a major test to take?

thoughts. The great part is, all you need is a quiet room in which to sit still and maybe a picture of yourself in a winning moment or at a time when you felt really good about yourself.

Try it out: Sit in a quiet place and think of a scene or look at the picture and relive the moment when it was taken. Then, close your eyes. Focus only on the event or image for as long as you can. Breathe deeply and evenly, and when distracted thoughts start trying to crowd their way in, push them away by thinking of that moment or image again. If thinking of nature, what about this scene makes you feel so relaxed? Think that you will always feel as peaceful as you do now. If using a photo, what sounds were happening at the time this picture was taken? Who was there? What made you feel so great at that time? Try to put yourself there and imagine that you will always be as successful as you were in that moment.

Dealing with Symptoms of Anxiety

We've all experienced it—the sweaty palms, the racing heart and dry mouth, and maybe even trouble breathing when we're anxious. If you experience this a lot, you might want to try doing yoga or muscle relaxation and breathing relaxation exercises.

Try it out: Yoga, an ancient Indian practice, will immediately teach you to concentrate on centering yourself and focus specifically on certain parts of the body. Your teacher will take you through asanas—movements that honor the natural state of the body's energy. These movements are performed slowly, and they will make you slow down, stretch, breathe, become aware of your body, and improve your flexibility.

Before your next big presentation in class or college interview, take a deep breath or two. Try the following deep-breathing technique: take a deep breath through your nose, and think about it as it travels through your body. Let your belly expand naturally, and then slowly exhale through your mouth. You may want to count as you do this to make sure you're slowing down, or imagine your breath as one long colored string that is moving in and out of your body.

Then try relaxing the muscles where tension is usually stored—in the neck, arms, and face. First inhale and make fists, and then clench every muscle on the way from your hands to your head—your forearms, shoulders, neck, jaw, and facial and eyelid muscles. Hold for the count of two, and then let go, exhaling deeply. This will let go of stored tension in these areas and will make you aware of where you were holding your emotions.

Yoga, meditation, and breathing exercises are all helpful ways to release tension. It also can be relaxing to spend time outdoors in a place you enjoy.

Dealing with Task-Related Worries

Sometimes when we are anxious about performing well academically, especially on tests and quizzes, we form bad habits that sap our energy and make us more nervous. If you tend to read and reread a hard question, check the clock every few minutes, peel your nail polish off, or sharpen and resharpen your pencil during tests, you're doing things that are what the Cornell University Center for Learning and Teaching calls task-generated interference. These are behaviors that actually make it harder for you to focus on the questions and eat away at any time you might use to answer questions and be successful in the situation.

Try it out: To fight these habits you've formed, work with an expert. Find a study skills instructor whose job it is to help students plan an order and a pattern of answering harder test questions. This study skills counselor might be in your school's resource room or at an after-school program, and he or she can help you identify specific behaviors that are tripping you up and create a plan to change or reduce these behaviors.

Dealing with Study Skills Problems

Sometimes it's not your test-taking habits, but your study habits that are problematic. You might have some study skills deficits. Study skills deficits are defined by the Cornell University Center for Learning and Teaching as "problems with your current study methods which create anxiety." This means that your anxiety

If you have trouble concentrating during a test, you might want to talk to a study skills counselor or instructor. He or she can help you learn effective study and test-taking habits.

might come from some less-than-great study habits that aren't allowing you to take in the information you need to do well. You might be reading the wrong parts of descriptions in your textbooks, or focusing on too many details or not enough details about new information. You might be missing key vocabulary in your reading. You might be studying at the last minute and trying to take in too much information, resulting in you not knowing

A study skills specialist, tutor, teacher, or even a parent may be able to assist you in organizing and prioritizing your time, and he or she can help you with challenging assignments.

answers to test questions, or you might be taking poor notes during class that lead to you being confused about what the assignment is.

Try it out: Work with a study skills counselor to figure out which study habits aren't working and learn about ones that will work for you. Another strategy you could try is keeping a calendar of your deadlines and test dates. You also could make a daily list to keep track of your obligations. Both of these methods may help you manage time but also free up your memory and, thus, reduce stress.

Last, think about your emotions. If the emotional difficulties of feeling academic anxiety are getting to you, it's best to talk to someone else even before you reach out to a study skills counselor. Again, a study skills counselor is a person in your resource room or at an after-school program whose job it is to help students work on managing their time and finding the best methods of studying for tests. If the pressure to do well is coming at you from all sides, it can make you feel as if there is no one to talk to about your thoughts and fears about achieving in school. In addition to the strategies you can try, there are places to go to find help when the pressure mounts. Two great Web sites that can help with any feelings of inadequacy and depression you might have as a result of school pressures are www.depressedteens.com and www.sengifted.org.

five

HOW CAN I HELP A FRIEND OR SIBLING STRUGGLING WITH ACADEMIC ANXIETY?

If your friend or sibling is struggling with academic anxiety, you might be the best person to help him or her through the stress. Because you are close to this person's age, you can notice stressed-out behavior before any adults do, and you can sympathize because you're probably going through the same juggling act of classes, reports, and exams that he or she is. The first and smartest thing to do is to reach out to this person and kindly tell him or her that you notice his or her anxiety. If you're uncritical and nice about it, your friend or sibling will feel less alone and more willing to talk to you about his or her pressures.

The second smart move is to let this person know that there are ways of dealing, or coping, with these feelings. Let's look at some steps BAM!, a Centers for Disease

Control and Prevention (CDC) Web site, recommends for coping with stress.

Get a Move On

If you're stressed out or are looking to avoid the stress caused by schoolwork, the CDC recommends you get moving. Get away from your desk or off the couch and get some exercise. Aerobic activities like running, riding a bicycle, and in-line skating will get your heart rate going and will increase the flow of endorphins, the chemicals that make you feel great. Yoga is another activity that has been proven to beat stress, too, though it focuses on relaxing the mind and body, rather than getting the endorphins flowing. You might want to do aerobic activity and yoga in the same week to balance your approach to fighting stress.

Eat to Beat Stress

The CDC recommends that you eat properly. Every nutritionist will tell you that it's important to start the day with a healthful breakfast that contains protein, fiber, and vitamins from fruit or fortified cereal. Eating breakfast gets your body primed for working all day, and eating regular meals keeps your blood sugar from dipping too low or soaring high, and then crashing during the day. Sitting down to eat a meal rather than grabbing snacks or food on the go, also will make you feel more relaxed. It can be stressful to munch and run, which is an all-too-common habit of teenagers in today's world.

Physical activity is a tremendous stress reliever. Biking, running, dancing, basketball, or any other form of exercise—even walking around the block—can help blow off some steam.

Laughter: The Best Medicine

When possible, laugh it off. It's important to take schoolwork seriously, but not so seriously that it affects your mind and spirit's wellness. Laughing is a way to let off steam, and its positive effects can last for hours after you've stopped laughing. According to the CDC, it takes fifteen facial muscles to laugh, which is good exercise for your spirit as well as your face. Talk to your funniest friend or relative, or find movies and books that crack you up.

Smiling and laughing have positive effects. Facial expressions actually contribute to what and how you're feeling. If, for example, you're not so happy but smile anyway, your mood will improve regardless.

Hang Out with Friends

Your friends can make your worries seem lighter just by sharing in the same stresses that you do. They sit next to you in class, take the same tests, work on the same projects, and know exactly what you are facing every day at school. Even if they go to another school, friends can engage you in activities that take your mind off your classroom worries. You're each other's own talking and sharing network.

Unpack Your Bag of Worries

Don't be afraid to share your worries with someone other than your friends. The CDC recommends that you talk out your problems with someone you trust to help see them from a different angle, before these feelings feel like a soda bottle about to blow its top off.

Zone Out

When academic anxiety feels like it's kicking you in the stomach, the CDC suggests that you find activities that help you zone out in a positive way. Listening to inspirational music, walking in the woods, working outside for a bit, painting, knitting, or baking are great ways to refocus your energy. These are great activities for a Saturday afternoon, or when stepping away from a homework assignment for a few minutes to clear your head.

Taking time during the day to do something you enjoy—such as playing or listening to music, reading, cooking, or drawing—is a good way to relax and refocus.

Count Sheep

When you're tired, every molehill seems like a mountain, and every mountain feels like you couldn't possibly climb it. Try to get the doctor-recommended eight hours of sleep each night. It only makes sense to hit the sack in time to prevent these feelings.

Write It Down

The CDC recommends putting your stressed-out thoughts and worries down on paper to let go of negative thoughts. Once you get the stress down on paper, you also could create a section of a journal for dreams and goals to look ahead.

Get Organized

Work always feels more manageable when it's compartmentalized. Put your different assignments into folders that are color-coded for each class, like green for English and red for science. Just think: organizing notes and papers can eliminate the stress of trying to find everything the night before a big test.

Help a Stressed-Out Peer

Share these ideas with your friend or sibling so that he or she can begin to realize that others are affected by the same feelings and that his or her anxiety can be fixed, or at least made smaller by working on it. As a resource, you can direct your friend or

Everything seems more challenging when you are tired. Getting enough sleep is an important first step to combating stress and anxiety.

sibling to www.bam.gov to take a stress quiz and read about other ways to cope with academic anxiety. After sharing these tips, you should suggest that he or she still "spill to someone you trust" in the adult world. You are a fantastic friend or sibling for already noticing and taking all the right steps to help the person you love, but adults also can step in if your friend's or sibling's anxiety becomes bigger or lasts longer than a few days.

Glossary

academic anxiety Worries, nervousness, or fears that occur from school pressures.

adrenaline Also known as epinephrine, this hormone is secreted by the adrenal glands located just above each kidney. This hormone is released when the amygdala sends a signal as part of the fight-or-flight response.

amygdala The almond-shaped part of the brain that controls fear and aggression and sends the signal to the body to release adrenaline for the fight-or-flight response.

anxiety Worry, nervousness, or fears.

anxiety disorder A psychiatric disorder in which a person feels anxiety that doesn't go away.

cope To deal well with a problem or a difficult situation.

dopamine The chemical compound in the brain that gets released into the blood just before adrenaline in the fight-or-flight response. The amygdala also is responsible for sending the signal that releases this chemical.

fight-or-flight response The body's chemical response to stress that starts with a signal from the amygdala, the part of the brain that controls fear and aggression. The amygdala signals the body to release the chemical adrenaline and slow down production of dopamine. This surge of chemicals makes the senses sharper and makes the body respond more quickly to danger while making it less apt to feel pain. In cases of physical danger, this response can make a person stay and fight the source of danger or run away from it.

learning style The way in which an individual learns best and most effectively processes information.

mental health professional Someone who has been trained to recognize and treat the emotions and behaviors that come with mental health problems.

obsessive-compulsive disorder (OCD) An anxiety disorder in which people are troubled by persistent, upsetting thoughts (obsessions), such as the fear of dirt or germs. They deal with this by developing rituals (compulsions), with which they try to control the fear. Someone who has OCD and suffers from the fear of contamination might wash his or her hands so many times a day that the hands become inflamed and bleed, and yet the idea of stopping fills the person with terror.

phobia A very powerful fear and dislike of something that isn't realistic, such as a fear of wide-open spaces or spiders.

psychiatrist A medical doctor who is licensed to treat people with mental health disorders, such as an anxiety disorder or an obsessive-compulsive disorder. He or she can prescribe medicine to treat these disorders; a psychologist cannot.

psychologist A professional who studies human behavior and has a license to provide psychotherapy.

psychotherapy Usually just called "therapy," this is the psychological treatment of emotional and behavioral problems. A psychologist, trained counselor, psychotherapist, or psychologist can give this type of therapy.

American MENSA, Ltd.

1229 Corporate Drive West

Arlington, TX 76006-6103

(817) 607-0060

Web site: http://www.us.mensa.org

American MENSA hosts links to a huge set of resources, including bookstores that carry books about managing stress for gifted children, organizations for gifted children and their parents, and a list of facts about being gifted.

BAM! Body and Mind

Centers for Disease Control and Prevention

1600 Clifton Road, MS C-04

Atlanta, GA 30333

(404) 639-3311

Web site: http://www.bam.gov

This Web site has articles for teenagers about managing stress, and social and health issues. It also provides links to other great resources.

The Center for Learning and Teaching

Cornell University

420 CCC, Garden Avenue Extension

Ithaca, NY 14853-6601

(607) 255-6310

Web site: http://www.clt.cornell.edu/campus/learn/
   SSWorkshops/SKResources.html
   The Study Skills Resources section of this Web site offers a
   wealth of tips about academic anxiety as well as study skills,
   and time and stress management.

National Institute of Mental Health

Public Information and Communications Branch

6001 Executive Boulevard, Room 8184, MSC 9663

Bethesda, MD 20892-9663

(866) 615-6464

Web site: http://www.nimh.nih.gov
   This Web site provides reliable health information, including
   kinds of anxiety disorders and additional mental health
   information for children and teens.

Nemours Foundation

The Nemours Center for Children's Health Media

252 Chapman Road, Suite 200

Newark, DE 19702

(302) 444-9100

Web site: http://www.kidshealth.org/teen
   This Web site has a great section specifically for teens that
   describes health issues that affect teenagers most frequently,
   including anxiety and related disorders.

Web Sites

Due to the changing nature of Internet links, Rosen Publishing has developed an online list of Web sites related to the subject of this book. This site is updated regularly. Please use this link to access the list:

http://www.rosenlinks.com/faq/acan

Friel, John C., Ph.D., and Linda D. Friel, M.A. *The 7 Best Things Smart Teens Do.* Deerfield Beach, FL: HCI Teens, 2000.

Garcia, Cara L. *Too Scared to Learn: Overcoming Academic Anxiety.* Thousand Oaks, CA: Corwin Press, 2002.

McGraw, Jay. *Life Strategies for Teens.* New York, NY: Fireside Press, 2000.

Merrell, Kenneth W. *Helping Students Overcome Depression and Anxiety: A Practical Guide.* New York, NY: The Guilford Press, 2001.

Seaward, Brian, and Linda Bartlett. *Hot Stones and Funny Bones: Teens Helping Teens Cope with Stress and Anger.* Deerfield Beach, FL: HCI Teens, 2002.

Sluke, Sara Jane, and Vanessa Torres. *The Complete Idiot's Guide to Dealing with Stress for Teens.* New York, NY: Alpha Books, 2001.

Bibliography

Centers for Disease Control and Prevention: BAM! Body
and Mind. "Feelin' Frazzled . . .?" Retrieved February
2007 (http://www.bam.gov/sub_yourlife/yourlife_
feelingfrazzled.html).

Cornell University Center for Learning and Teaching. Study
Skills Resources: "Understanding Academic Anxiety" and
"Letting Go of Text Anxiety." Retrieved February 2007
(http://www.clt.cornell.edu/campus/learn/SSWorkshops/
SKResources.html#Stress).

DeBord, Karen, Ph.D. "Helping Children Cope with Stress."
National Network for Child Care. 1996. Retrieved
February 2007 (http://www.ces.ncsu.edu/depts/fcs/
human/pubs/copestress.html).

A Family Guide to Keeping Youth Mentally Healthy and
Drug Free. "Spring Scheduling." May 16, 2003. Retrieved
February 2007 (http://family.samhsa.gov/get/school_
community/scheduling.aspx).

Girl Power! "BodyWise: Stress." Retrieved February 2007
(http://www.girlpower.gov/girlarea/bodywise/bodyimage/
stress.htm).

Girl Power! "Journaling: A Place for Your Private Thoughts
and Personal Dreams!" Retrieved February 2007 (http://
www.girlpower.gov/girlarea/general/journaling.htm).

Hack, Sabine, M.D. "Stress in Children: What It Is and How
    Parents Can Help." AboutOurKids.org. May 15, 2001.
    Retrieved February 2007 (http://www.aboutourkids.org/
    articles/stress.html).

Hendrickson, Gail, RN, BS. "Stress." Discovery Health:
    Diseases & Conditions Database. Retrieved February 2007
    (http://health.discovery.com/diseasesandcond/encyclopedia/
    3096.html).

Kessler, R. C., P. A. Berglund, O. Demler, R. Jin, and E. E.
    Walters. "Lifetime Prevalence and Age-of-Onset Distributions
    of DSM-IV Disorders in the National Comorbidity Survey
    Replication (NCS-R)." *Archives of General Psychiatry*,
    Vol. 62, No. 6, June 2005, pp. 593–602.

Kessler, R. C., W. T. Chiu, O. Demler, and E. E. Walters.
    "Prevalence, Severity, and Comorbidity of Twelve-Month
    DSM-IV Disorders in the National Comorbidity Survey
    Replication (NCS-R)." *Archives of General Psychiatry*,
    Vol. 62, No. 6, June 2005, pp. 617–627.

Klein, Karin, Ed.D. "Parent Connection: Learning to Laugh."
    Pre-K Smarties. Retrieved February 2007 (http://www.
    preksmarties.com/connection/connectionSept2.htm).

MedlinePlus. "Anxiety." Retrieved February 2007
    (http://www.nlm.nih.gov/medlineplus/anxiety.html).

Milgram N., and Y. Toubiana. "Academic Anxiety, Academic
    Procrastination, and Parental Involvement in Students and
    Their Parents." *British Journal of Educational Psychology*,
    Vol. 69, No. 3, September 1999, pp. 345–361(17).

National Association for Gifted Children. "Information and Resources: Frequently Used Terms in Gifted Education." Retrieved February 2007 (http://www.nagc.org/CMS400Min/index.aspx?id=565).

National Center for Farm Worker Health. "Tips to Reduce Stress." Retrieved February 2007 (http://www.ncfh.org/pateduc/en-stress.htm).

National Institute of Mental Health. "The Numbers Count: Mental Disorders in America." 2006. Retrieved February 2007 (http://www.nimh.nih.gov/publicat/numbers.cfm#KesslerLifetime).

Scott, Elizabeth, M.S. "How to Reduce Student Stress and Excel in School." About.com. Retrieved February 2007 (http://stress.about.com/od/studentstress/ht/schoolstress.htm?terms=academic+anxiety).

Tullis, Debra. "Coping with Test and Academic Anxiety." ClickEducation.info. December 6, 2005. Retrieved February 2007 (http://www.clickeducation.info/coping-with-test-and-academic-anxiety/).

University of Illinois Extension: Helping Children Succeed in School. "School Stress." Retrieved February 2007 (http://www.urbanext.uiuc.edu/succeed/03-stress.html).

Zolten, Kristen, M.A., and Nicholas Long, Ph.D. "Helping Children Cope with Stress." Center for Effective Parenting. 1997. Retrieved February 2007 (www.parenting-ed.org/handout3/Specific%20Concerns%20and%20Problems/kid%20stress.htm).

Index

Photo Credits

Cover © www.istockphoto.com/Joshua Blake; p. 5 © Syracuse Newspapers/The Image Works; pp. 7, 26, 48, 51 Shutterstock.com; p. 10 © www.istockphoto.com/Diane Diederich; p. 18 © www.istockphoto.com/geotrac; p. 20 © www.istockphoto.com/diego cervo; p. 24 © Mary Kate Denny/PhotoEdit; p. 29 © Eastcott-Momatiuk/The Image Works; p. 32 © www.istockphoto.com/Andrew Rich; p. 33 © Getty Images; p. 36 © Dana White/PhotoEdit; p. 41 © www.istockphoto.com/blindelinse; p 43 © www.istockphoto.com/Laurence Gough; p. 44 © Ellen B. Senisi/The Image Works; p. 49 © www.istockphoto.com/Pascal Genest; p. 53 © Peter Byron/PhotoEdit.

Series Designer: Evelyn Horovicz
Photo Researcher: Cindy Reiman